TopReaders

The Greeks

Robert Coupe

Contents

For many centuries in ancient times Greece was a very powerful country. In some ways, ancient Greeks were like us. Read more about them here.

New Settlements

Ancient Greek civilization began on islands in the Aegean Sea . By 2,700 years ago, Greeks had spread out to other lands, where they set up colonies . They built many fine new cities.

Greeks made new settlements near the sea. They built cities and temples like those they had at home.

Fact File

Greeks created colonies in parts of countries that we now call Turkey, Bulgaria, Romania, Italy, France, and Spain.

What They Wore

Greeks wore garments called tunics.
These were large pieces of material
that they wrapped around their bodies.
In summer they often went barefoot.
Rich people sometimes wore fine jewelry.

Women's Tunics

Women wore two main types of tunics. One
was usually wool. The other was mainly linen.

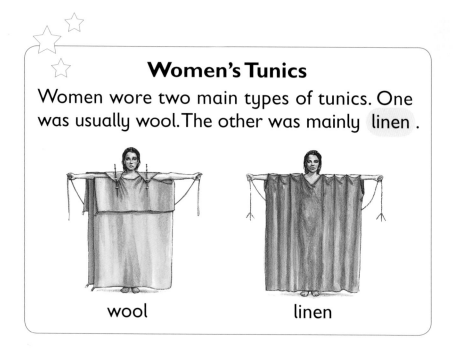

| wool | linen |

*In winter, people covered their summer tunics with warm
cloaks. They wore wide hats to protect them from the sun.*

Meeting Place

A Greek city had a central open space.
This place was called the agora .
Public meetings and markets
were held there.

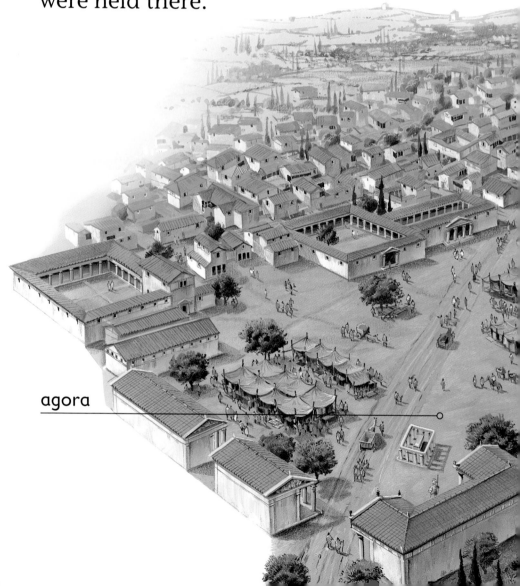

agora

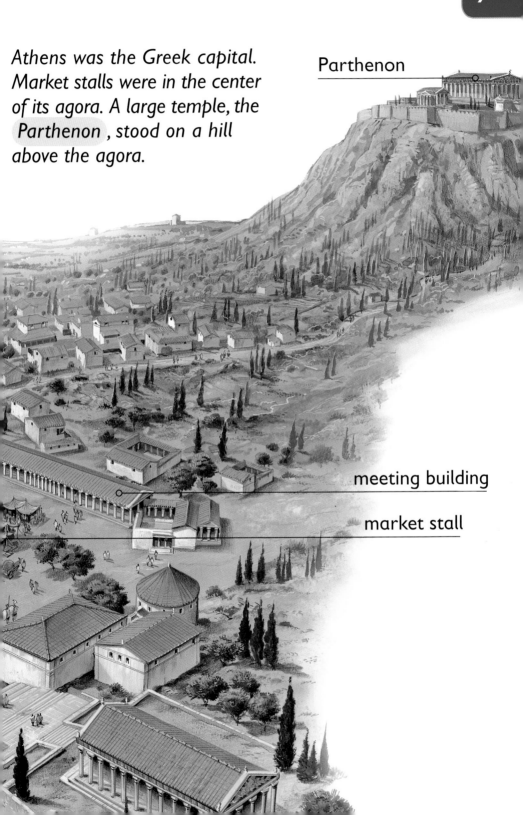

Athens was the Greek capital.
Market stalls were in the center
of its agora. A large temple, the
Parthenon , stood on a hill
above the agora.

Parthenon

meeting building

market stall

Products such as wine and olive oil were carried on ships in large pots called amphorae. Can you see them in the picture?

Trade

Athens was an important trade center. Goods coming to Athens arrived at the port of Piraeus. This port was about 4 miles (6 km) from the city. A large wall surrounded its harbor.

Fact File

Most of the grain that Athens needed to feed its people was brought into Piraeus by ship from Egypt and other parts of Greece.

Pots and Vases

Many thousands of pots and vases
from ancient Greece still exist.
Potters prepared a liquid clay
called slip . They used this
to decorate the pots.

Fact File

The decorations on Greek vases
tell stories about gods and
heroes. They also show pictures
of everyday actions and objects.

*Many potters and other craftspeople worked in
buildings along the sides of the agora in Athens.*

Health and Fitness

Keeping fit was important to the Greeks. People went to gymnasiums to exercise and practice sports. To cure diseases, Greek doctors often used medicines they made from herbs.

Herbs as Medicines

Doctors used hyssop and mullein to treat coughs, and motherwort to ease pain.

hyssop   mullein   motherwort

Doctors thought that if a sick person was made to bleed, sickness would leave the body. This doctor has taken blood from a child's arm.

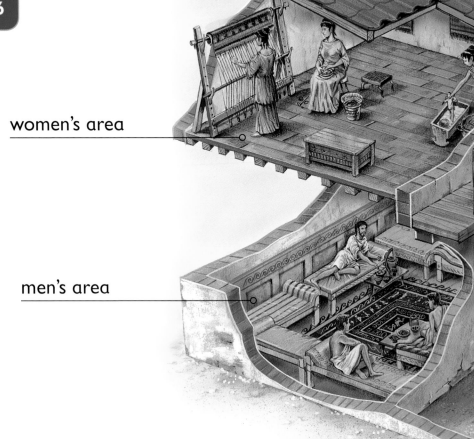

women's area

men's area

At Home

Greek houses had walls of mud bricks.
Their roofs were made of pottery tiles.
In the center was an open courtyard.
In this courtyard was an altar where
the family prayed to their gods.

central
courtyard

Rich people had male and female slaves *who helped them with the cooking and all the other housework.*

Rich Greek men held feasts, called symposiums *. Slaves served food and wine, and young women danced and played music.*

Eating and Drinking

Much of Greece is hot and dry.
Many crops were hard to grow.
Grapes for wine and olives grew well
on hillsides, but for a long time wheat
was imported from Egypt and other places.

☆ Party Food

Food at symposiums included roasted birds, mushrooms, snails, and tuna fish. Bread was always served. Greeks ate it with olive oil.

At School

Only sons of rich parents went to school.
Some girls learned reading and writing
at home. When they were 18, young men
were taught to fight, so they could be soldiers.

Fact File

Boys learned to play the lyre, which had strings and pipes, which they blew into like a flute.

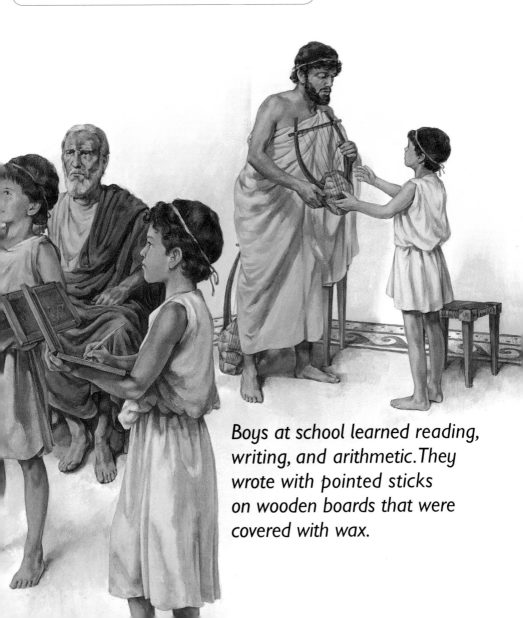

Boys at school learned reading, writing, and arithmetic. They wrote with pointed sticks on wooden boards that were covered with wax.

Theater

Some Greek plays told serious stories.
Other plays, called comedies, were funny.
Only men acted in plays. They wore masks.

Greeks watched and listened to plays in large open-air theaters. The spectators' seats rose above the stage.

Working

Many ancient Greeks worked hard.
Others, who were rich, did not need
to earn a living. They owned slaves
and paid laborers to work for them.

*People crushed grapes to make wine
by treading on them in vats.*

Fact File

Many slaves were captured in wars. Some slaves earned money and then paid to become free.

Building

Most buildings from ancient Greece have not lasted. Temples were built of stone or marble. You can still see these today in parts of Greece.

Columns

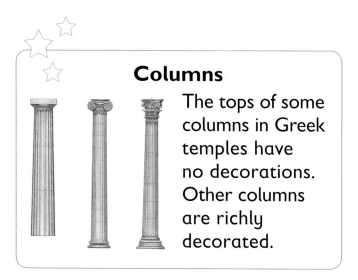

The tops of some columns in Greek temples have no decorations. Other columns are richly decorated.

Large statues of young women were used to support the roofs of many temples. These statues are called caryatids.

The Olympics

The Olympic Games began in Greece.
They were held every four years
after 776 BC at a place called Olympia.
The games lasted for five days.

Only men competed in the games at Olympia. Throwing a discus *was one of the most popular contests.*

Quiz

Can you unscramble the words and match them with the right pictures?

HEARTTE   LOMUNCS

GAROA   UCTIN

Glossary

Aegean Sea: part of the Mediterranean Sea that lies between Greece and Turkey

agora: an open space used for meetings and markets

amphorae: large jars that were used for storing and moving wine, olive oil, and fish sauce in ancient Greece

colonies: places that are settled and controlled by people from a more powerful country

discus: a flat, heavy, round object

linen: a strong cloth made from the fibers of flax plants

lyre: a stringed musical instrument like a small harp. A player held a lyre with one hand and plucked the strings with the other hand.

Olympia: a place in southern Greece where the first Olympic Games were held

Parthenon: a large temple in Athens

slaves: people who belong to someone else and are forced to work for them

slip: a thick liquid clay, used for painting vases and pots

spectators: people who are part of an audience

symposiums: feasts where ancient Greek men talked about important matters

temples: buildings where people worship or pray to a god or gods

Index